The Secrets of Photography
Part 1 Guide
By Tomer Burmad

Intro

Shooting captivating images is not conditioned with owning a pricy camera or having an array of high-end photography equipment. What matters is the photographer's point of view, the way he interacts with the visual subject he chose to capture and his use of the many skills & composition principals of photography.

Although it seems that certain photographers have innate abilities to shoot amazing photos, this ability usually comes from enthusiasm and passion along with the knowledge acquired by practicing experience.

The emphasis of this book is about the basis practice approach along with control over photography skills in different techniques in the subjects of: portrait, still life, scenery, architecture, nature & food accompanied with my work as reference.

My examples will show you the technical details, the equipment used, camera angles and a wide variety of specifics you can use to create amazing photos, based on my personal experience.

In order to shoot interesting, captivating photos, you need to get familiar with the different options your camera has. The more these options are implemented, more time to address composition and right timing of shooting is available. So, we already established that a good photo is a fascinating photo, a one that's delivering emotion, thought and conveying its own unique trades – subject, lines, materials & textures (for example, wood texture or ceramic), colors, light & shade, all necessary to deliver the feel of the subject & a 3D quality that brings life to a flat two-dimension image. Every photographer decides what trades are emphasized in his photo. Our equipment, lighting accessories gives us major flexibility and control, and photo retouching improves/adds what is 'missing' in the original shoot, all of these conditions allow us, as photographers, to reach better end results & produce high-end quality photographs.

In this book I will present you all of these options along with how to avoid common shooting mistakes. We will work on creativity & personal style by experimenting in a wide variety of photography options and discover the ways of which we can follow to a personal expression.

Just follow the instructions of each chapter and you are on your way to becoming a photography artist.

LESSON #1:

THE DIGITAL CAMERA INTRODUCTION

THE CAMERA STRUCTURE

SHUTTER SPEED

APERTURE ADJUSTER

FIELD DEPTH

EXPOSURE

COMPOSITION

CORRECT EXPOSURE

EXPOSURE COMPENSATION

PHOTOGRAPHY FUNCTIONS

TYPES OF LENS

WINDOW LIGHT

LIGHT MEASURING

LIGHT MEASURING OPTIONS

CORRECT EXPOSURE

DYNAMIC RANGE

HDR PHOTOGRAPHY

ISO

THE DIGITAL CAMERA:

Basic understanding of the camera's optic principals allows us to concentrate in the composition & lighting of each shoot.

If we were to remove the electronic & automatic technology case off of the camera, we would find the basic design - The camera is actually a box, sealed proof to light, with a hole on one hand, that on top of it a lens is assembled, and a light-sensitive motion sensor on the other hand to measure the amount of light reaching the sensor. Inside the lens there's an aperture that is adjustable for tuning and change the size of its adjuster opening.

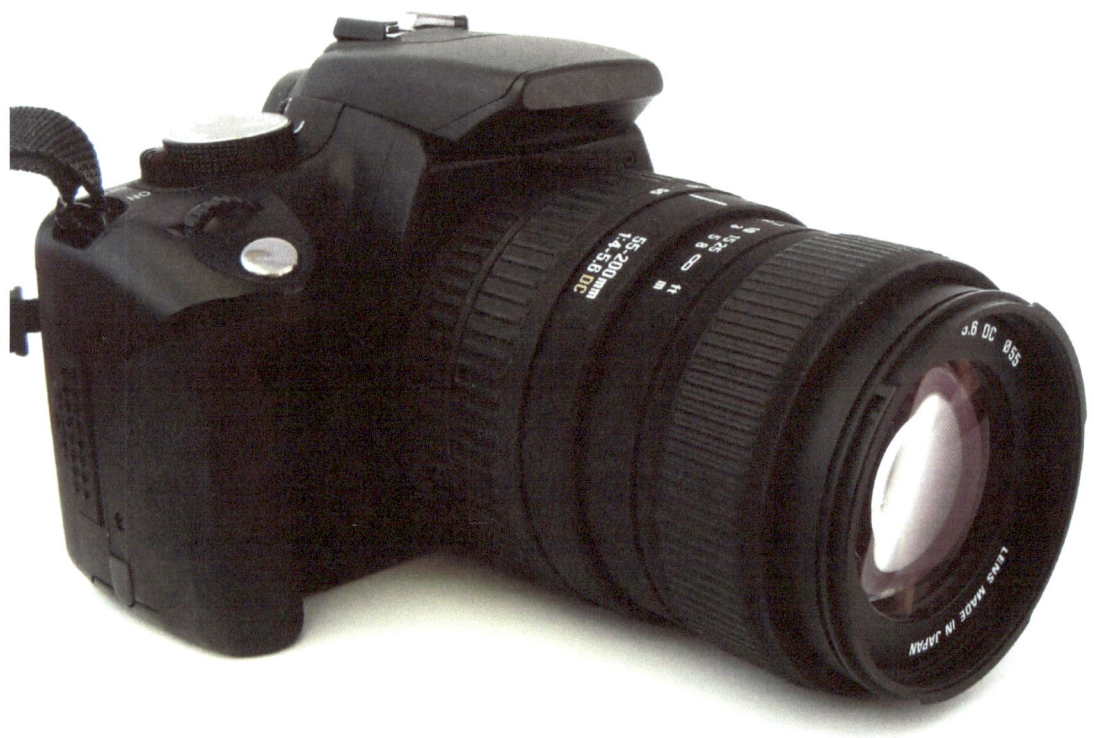

Light exposure time is what counts how much light reaches the sensor; exposure time is controllable by a shutter that allows the entry or blockage of light reaching the sensor. Good balance of shutter opening and closing creates good exposure (The aperture is made by a series of overlapping blades, creating a circle, that open when you press the shoot button. The shutter is made by delicate metal holders that move & open during exposure parallel to the sensor).

If we wish to freeze movement or create a movement blur, we will have to change the shutter speed & aperture opening up to the correct exposure. A dial or control light inside the camera viewfinder will mark good exposure:

Small aperture opening (F-16) – For large depth of field
Large aperture opening (F-4) – For small depth of field

A good balance of shutter speed and aperture opening allow us to achieve good exposure.

There is an important link between the two factors: Shutter speed & Aperture opening:

When you press on the shoot button (camera/shutter release) two technical features are triggered:

1. Shutter activation
2. Aperture activation

Partial press activates the light measure and the rest of the auto exposure system.
Full press activates the shutter closure.

The shutter, in most cameras, is located at the back side of the camera & triggering it sets the time frame where light enters the camera. Changing the shutter speed meaning changing the time frame where light enters the camera.

Shutter is marked as **TV** or **S**.

There are also alias names for the shutter (Closure or Fissile closure). Usually the shutter speed appears on the camera body, in digital cameras it appears on the control board. Speed appears in multiples where each number doubles its predecessor. On digital cameras speed range can grow, slowly up to 30 seconds, and a very high speed of up to 1/8000 per second.

When choosing a certain shutter speed with function TV/S, it will define the exposure with preferability to shutter speed and the aperture opening will fit itself to the speed chosen.

The aperture is located inside the camera lens and is built by a circle of fine metal overlapping blades, a structure also known as 'Diaphragm'.

The aperture is reducing light amount. It changes the lens aperture diameter and affects the amount of light entering the camera and the sharpness of the objects filmed.

With the camera wheel/ring on top of the lens you can adjust the aperture diameter of the lens.

Low aperture numbers increase the aperture diameter and letting more light in. High aperture numbers decrease the aperture diameter and reducing the amount of light.

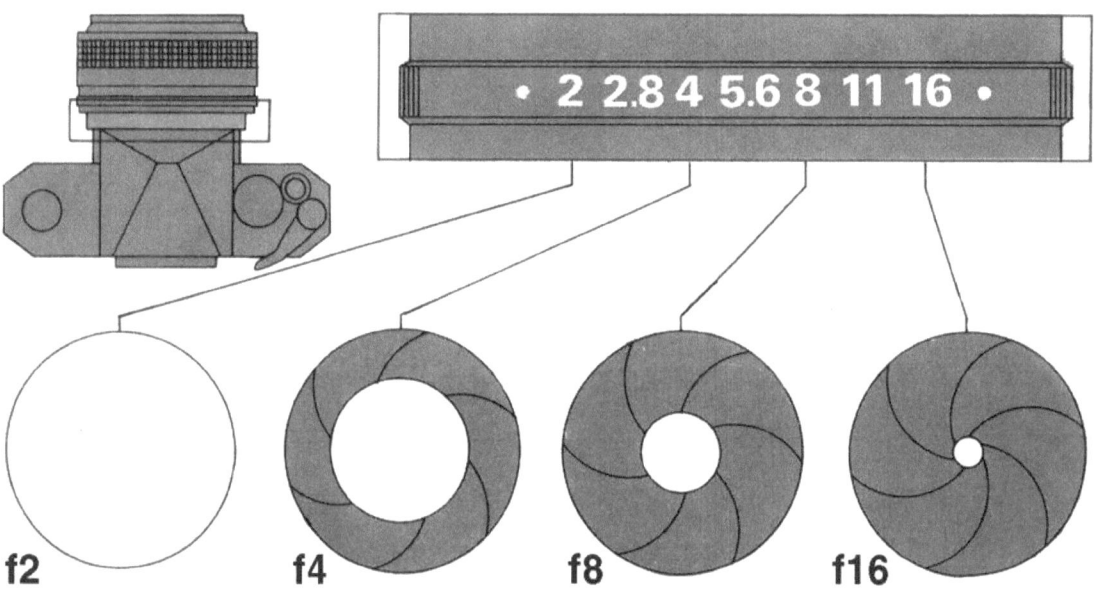

Depth of Field - Aperture range of sharpness

The main important action the use of aperture diameter allow is control over the sharpness of the shooting subjects.

The sharp range of objects/subjects of shooting is called 'Depth of Field' – the range between the nearest and the farthest object where objects seems sharp.

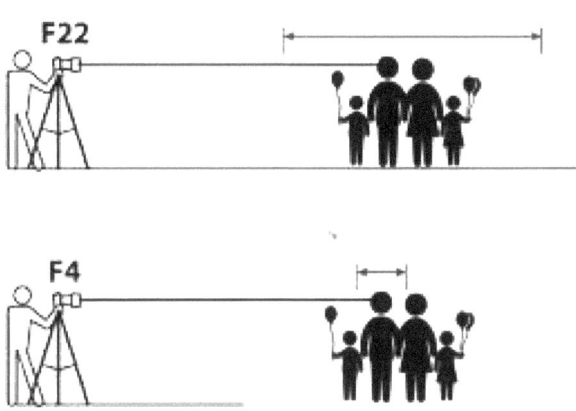

A high aperture number (F-16) reduces the lens diameter, this range increases the depth of field and by that increases sharpness, since the rays of light passing through the thin opening sharpen.

A small aperture number (F-4) enlarges the lens diameter, this range reduces the depth of field, meaning, lowering sharpness, since the rays of light passing through a wider opening & distribute.

The importance of the depth of field in photography expressed when shooting up-close in a range of 0.3 – 2 meters away, when shooting from a distance the subject/objects will always be in a reasonable sharpness.

When choosing a certain aperture within the AV/A function there will be preferability for the aperture and the shutter speed will adjust it to match. Inside the camera there is a light measure measuring the light rays bouncing back from the object of shooting and provides us with information of the exposure amount. The light measure basically determines the shutter speed for the shoot and the right exposure.

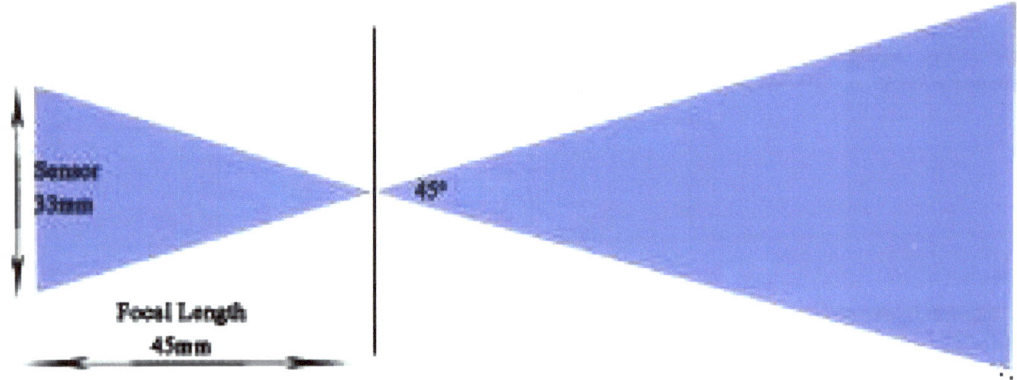

Aperture numbers represents lens opening diameter (aperture diameter) In relation to lens length. For example: if the lens length is 5 centimeters & the lens diameter opening is also 5 centimeters, than the lens will be defined as 1:1 or 1, if the lens focal length is 5 centimeters and the opening diameter is 2.5 centimeters – the lens will be defined 1:2 or 2, meaning the lens diameter opening is 2 times smaller than its length F=1:2 or F=2. From that we can include that if the marking of the lens indicates F=4 than the lens opening diameter is 4 times smaller than its length, F=22 meaning that the diameter opening is 22 times smaller than the lens length etc.

All aperture numbers indicates the lens opening diameter (aperture diameter) related to the lens length.

Lens Length Meaning:

Aperture numbers relate to lens length, lens length is one of the main features of the lens and defined by the name 'Focal length' or 'Distant focus' and marked by the letter **'F'**.

'Focal Length' influences on:

1. The lens vision angle
2. The size of the objects indicated by the sensor
3. Size relations between the near & far objects
4. Influence on the linear perspective of the objects

Defining the lens focal length:

The lens focal length is the distance between the optic centers of the lens to the sensor pallet when the lens is focused to infinity (∞). If we set the camera lens to the object 'infinity' distance the light rays hitting the lens & passing through it will parallel & meet at a certain point at the other side of the lens. The image we will get will be small & up-side down. The meeting point of the light rays on the sensor is called a 'focal point' whilst the distance from the camera's optic center to this point is called 'lens focal length'. Focal length is measured in millimeters, inches or centimeters & marked on the outer rim around the lens as 'F' with a number indicating the focal length of the specific lens.

Types of Lenses

There are two types of focal lengths:
1. A lens with a steady focal length.
2. A lens with an adjustable focal length (zoom lens).

Zoom Lens:

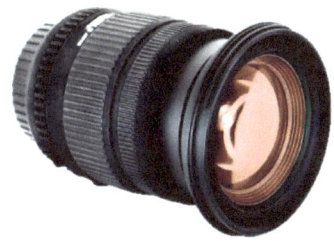

Steady Focal Length Lens:

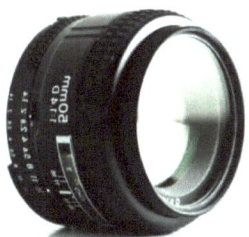

Zoom lens allows you to change the size of your object without moving the camera, a trait that makes this lens extremely popular among photographers (in compact cameras also installed zoom lenses).

We can divide the different lenses types into 3 groups:
1. wide angel
2. Standard
3. Long focal length

it's hard to determine certain focal lengths for each group since those set by the type & size of the camera.

Focal length of a standard lens equals to the object diagonal length as seen on the camera. Meaning, for a 35mm camera where the object's diagonal length is about 50mm, the focal length of a standard lens will be 50-55mm. on a camera such as this, an 80mm lens is considered to be Long-term focus.

DEPTH OF FIELD IN PHOTOGRAPHY
Important traits of the camera lens & its influence of the photoshoot

Focal length determines the object size as seen on the sensor (film) and influence over the linear (geometric) perspective.

On standard 35mm cameras the sensor's size is 36X24mm (3:4) focal length lens of F-50 will be defined as 'standard' (normal) and the viewpoint angle of this lens will be around 45 degrees (similar to the human eyesight angle).

With a focal length of over 50mm the lens will be defined as long focal length & short/small viewpoint, under 50mm the lens will be defined as short focal length & wide/large viewpoint.

The focal length influences also on objects size defined at 'infinity' distance. For example: if shooting with a 50mm focal length lens an object defined at infinity, the object will be photographed at 10mm size, and in a 100mm lens it will be displayed at a 20mm size, and in a 200mm lens at the size of 40mm. therefore, in a short focal length lenses the object will be smaller according to the focal length and the viewpoint will increase.

In conclusion, if shooting in a long focal length lens, the object will appear larger and looks as if shot up-close and vise-versa, in a short focal length lens the object will appear small and will look as if shot from afar.

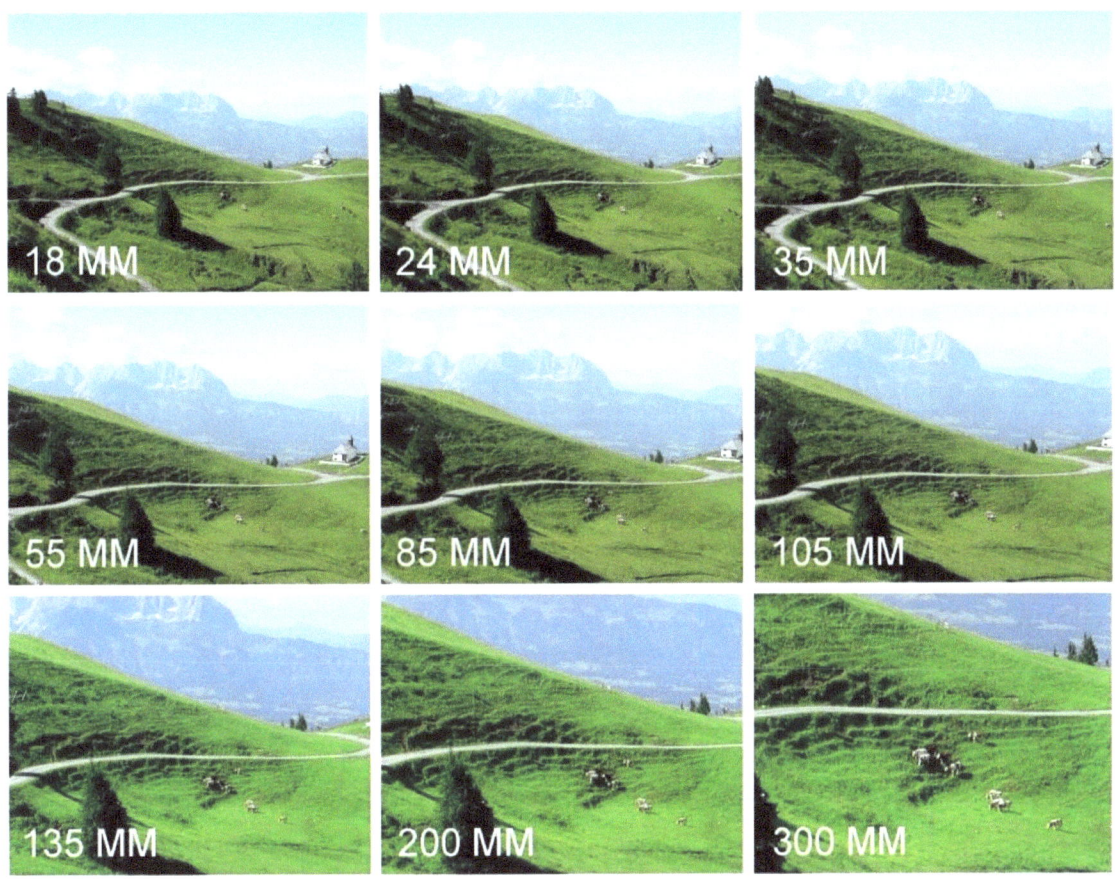

*You can see how the focal length and viewpoint angle affects the object size that is defined at infinity and appears in the final photo.

In case there is an object defined closer than infinity and we would like to have it in the same way it appears on a 'normal' lens, we will need to distant in a long focal length lens, and get closer in a short focal length lens. In both cases object size in infinity will not change – in the long focal length lens they will appear larger and the sense we will get in the photo is as if they are closer together. In a short focal length lens they will appear smaller and seem as if they are further apart. In both cases (long & short) we will get a distorted perspective.

COMPOSITION

Composition is basically building our photo, we decide what will be captured within the photo and what will be left out.

In photography art, composition is the product relationship between an object and the frame creation and also between the various objects within the creation.

When choosing the composition, the photographer places the objects to direct whoever is viewing the photo to the main features. For example, objects that create straight lines, diagonal or wavy can be used to draw the eye to the main centers.

Composition is built from the main theme, secondary & background common denominator:

1. Subject – the key element of the photo & will be clear to the viewer it's the theme.

2. Secondary Subject – will complement or competing with the key subject, contributing the viewer information or completing another angle on the subject.

3. Backdrop – the background completes the subject (pay attention it's not drawing too much attention from the subject). An appropriate backdrop is contributing a lot to the final photo & can make a reasonable photo into a great one.

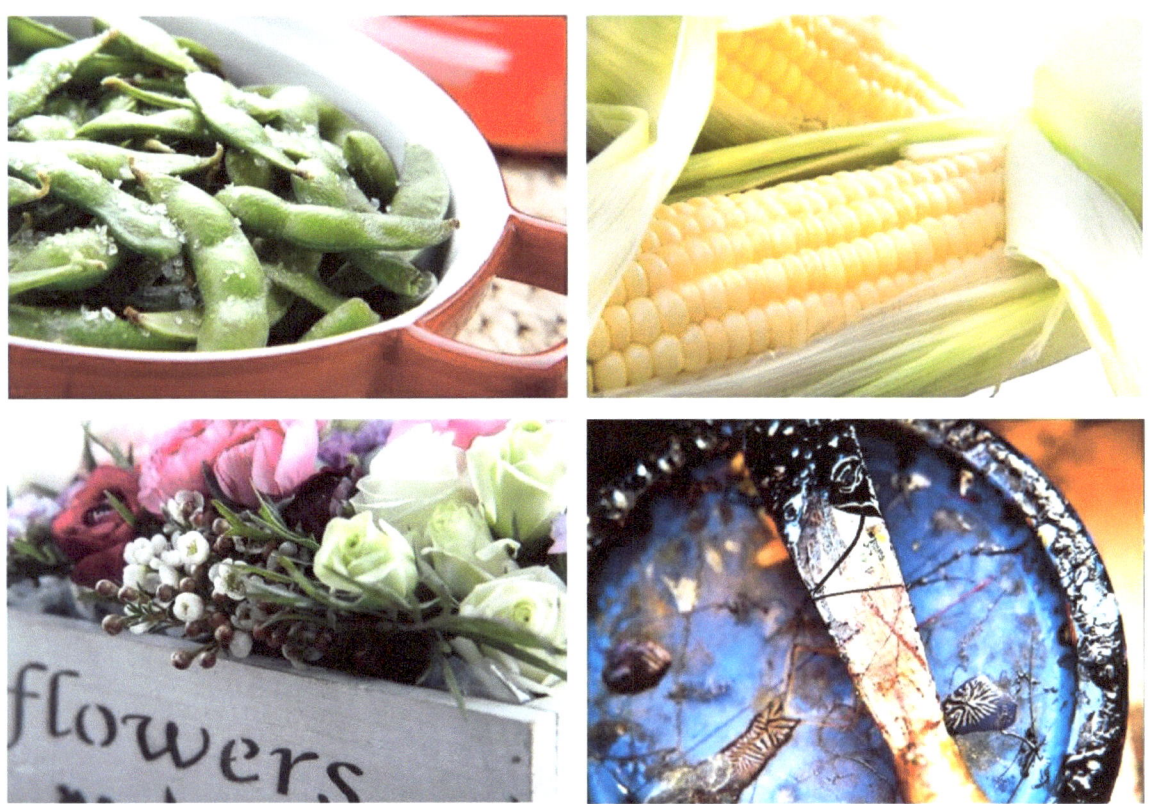

<u>The Rule of Thirds</u>

Dividing the frame (image) into 3 vertical thirds and 3 horizontal thirds;
The location of the objects on the photo over the divided thirds will create a far more interesting composition.

Examples:

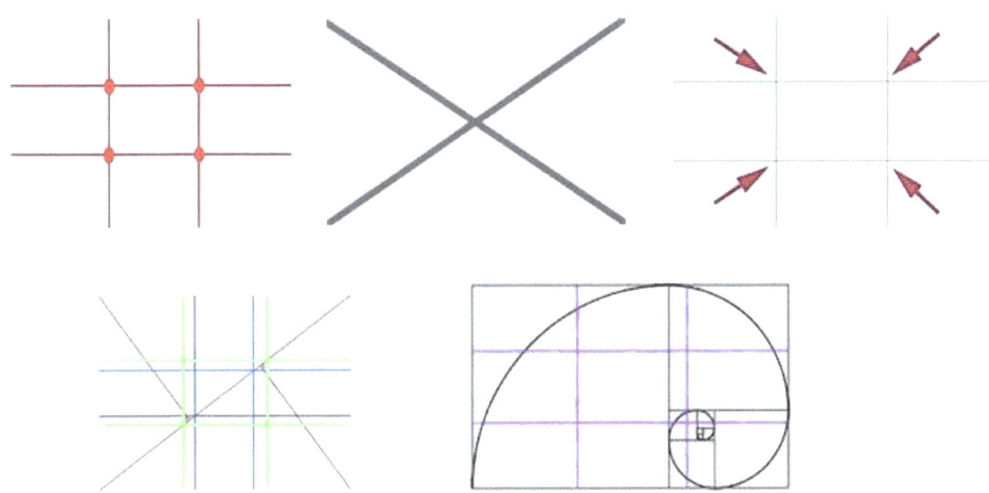

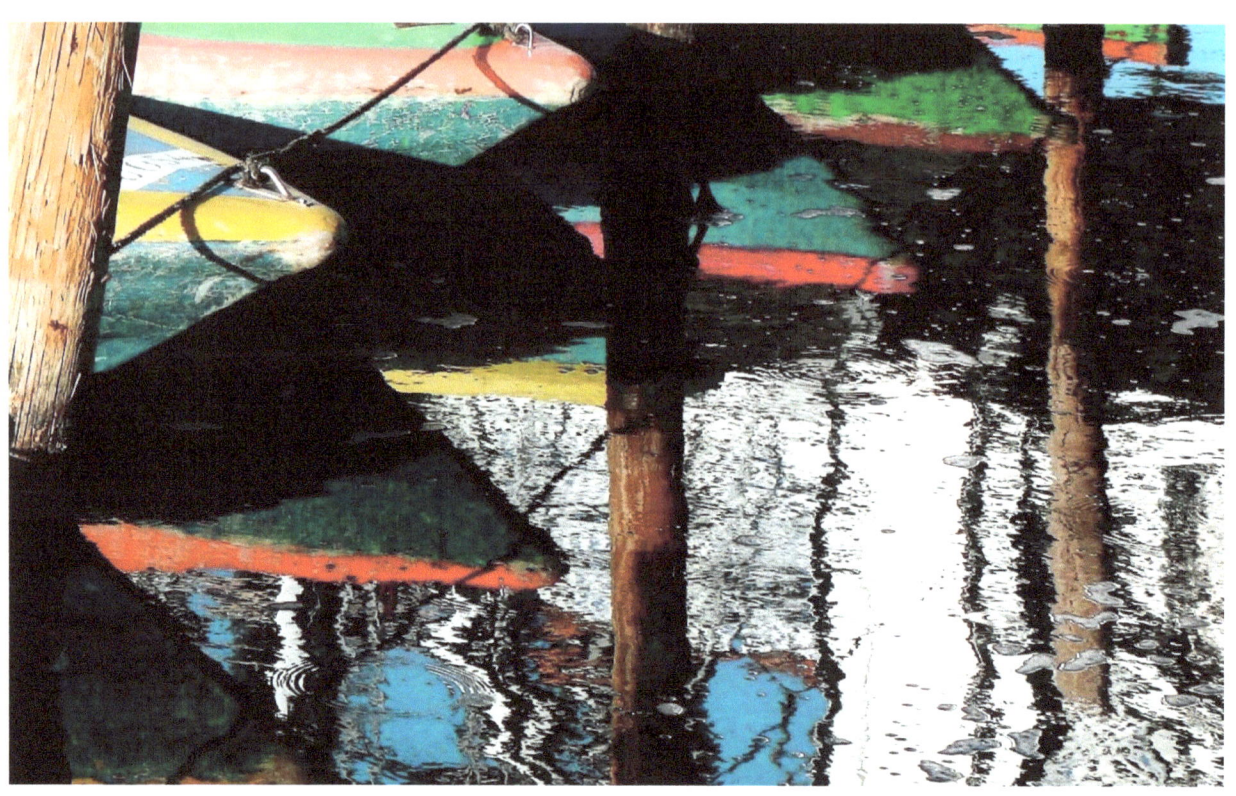

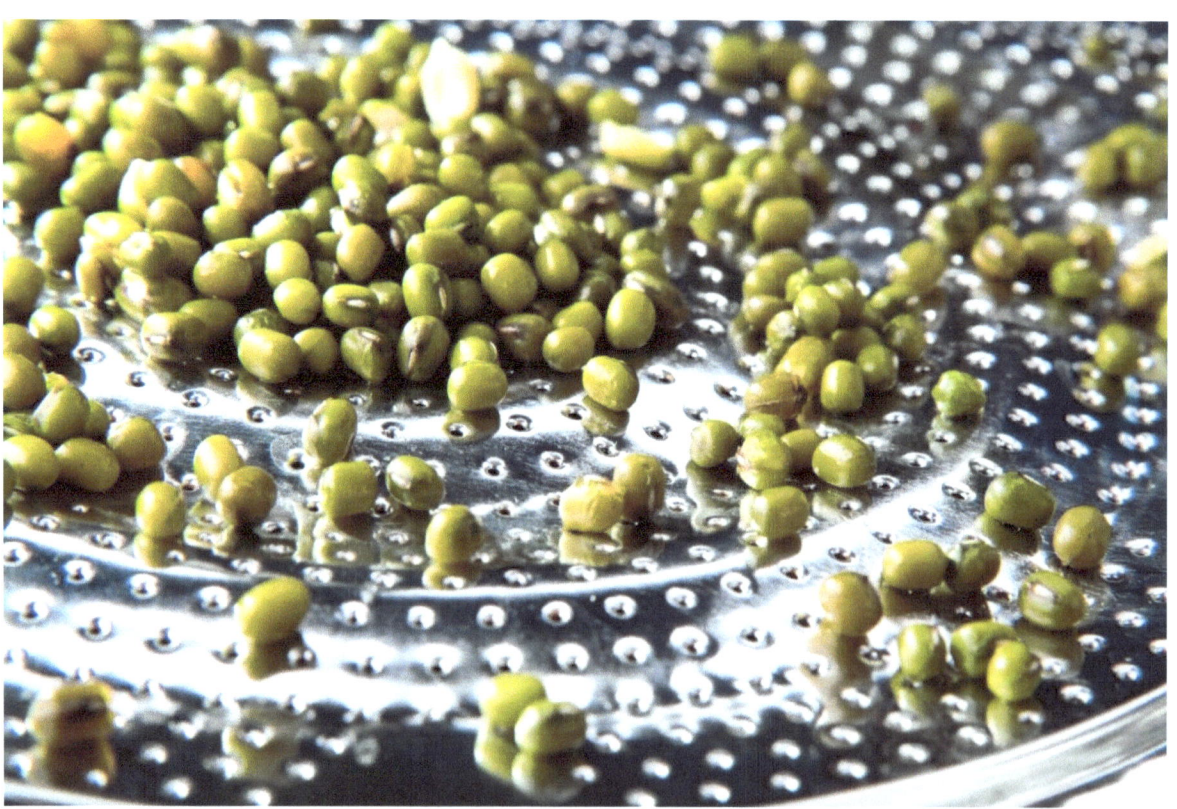

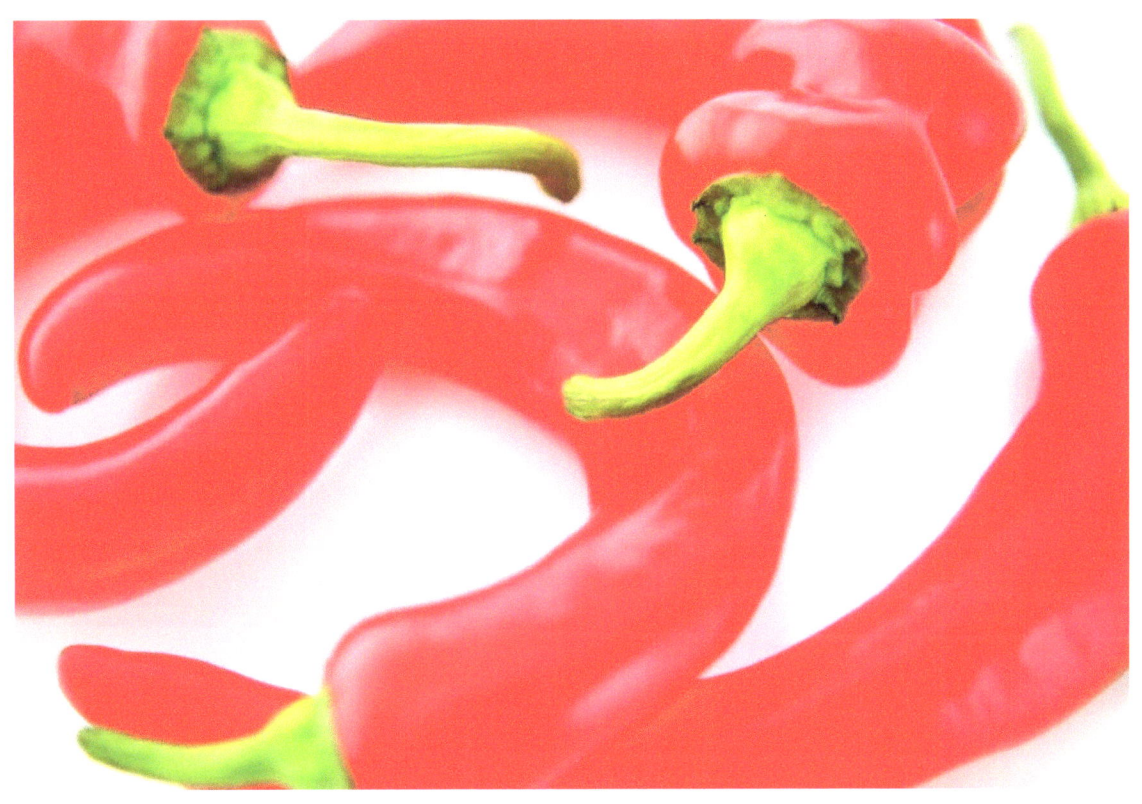

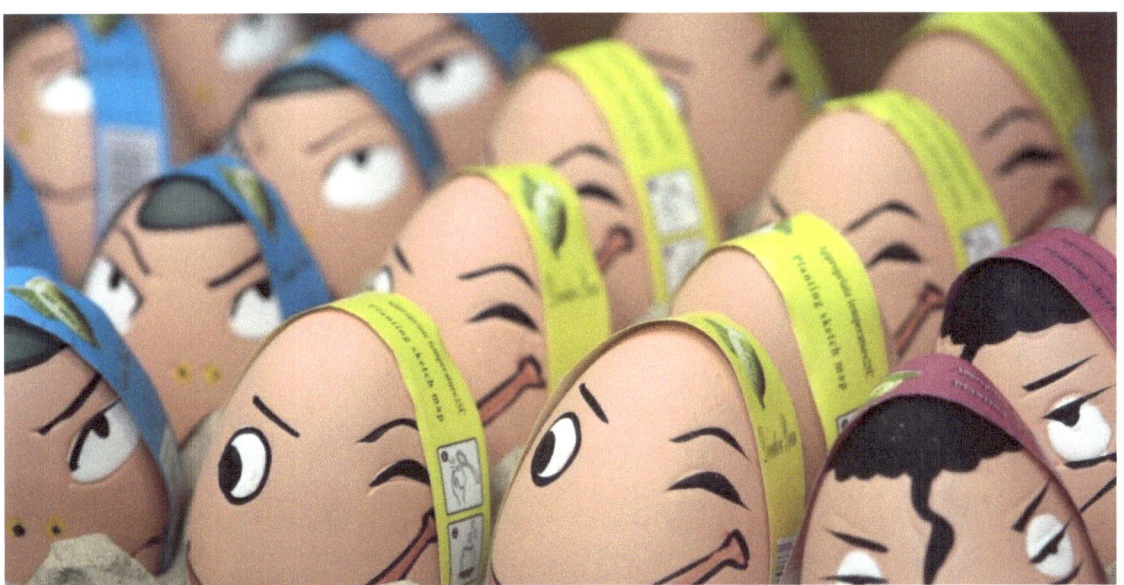

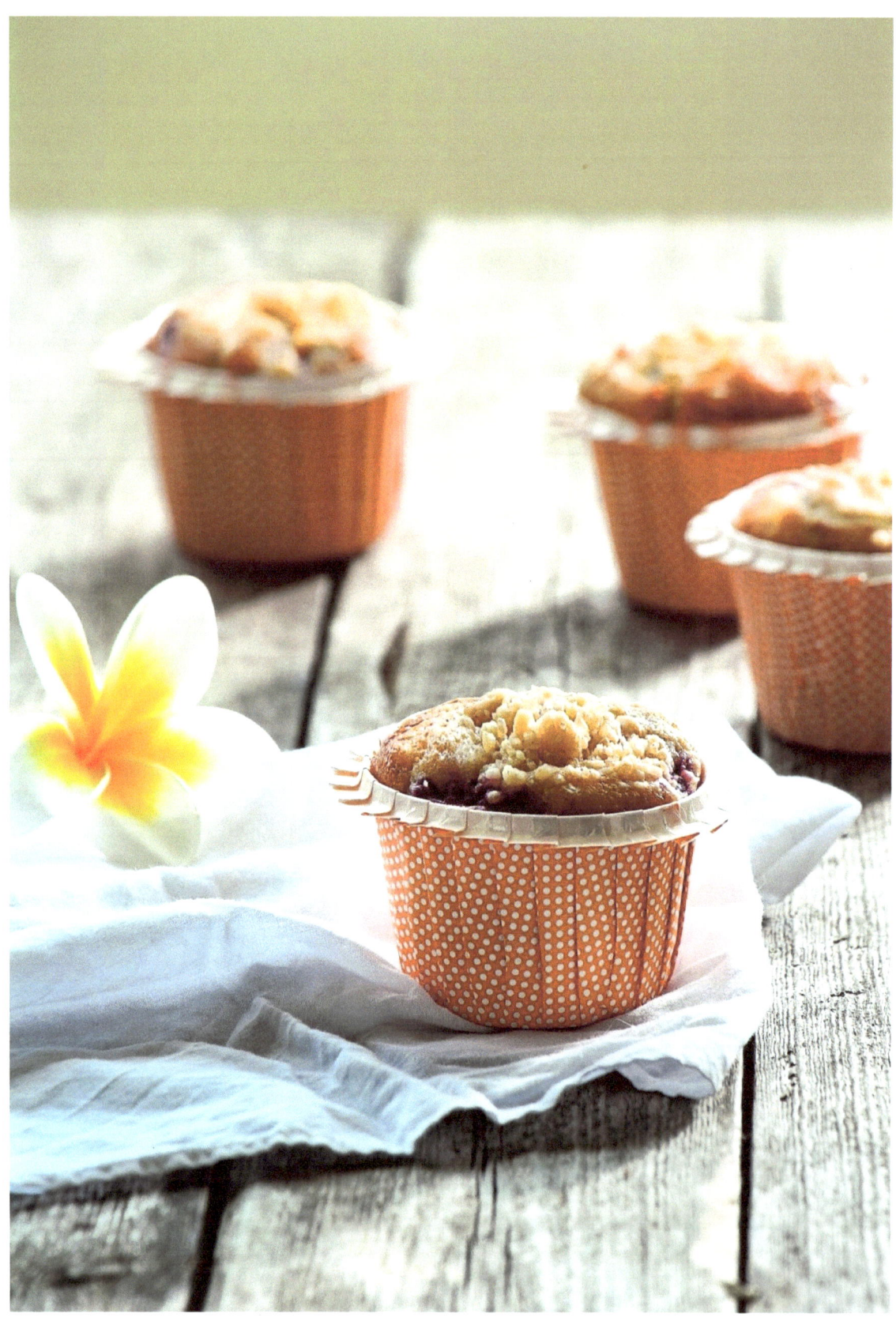

Natural closer:

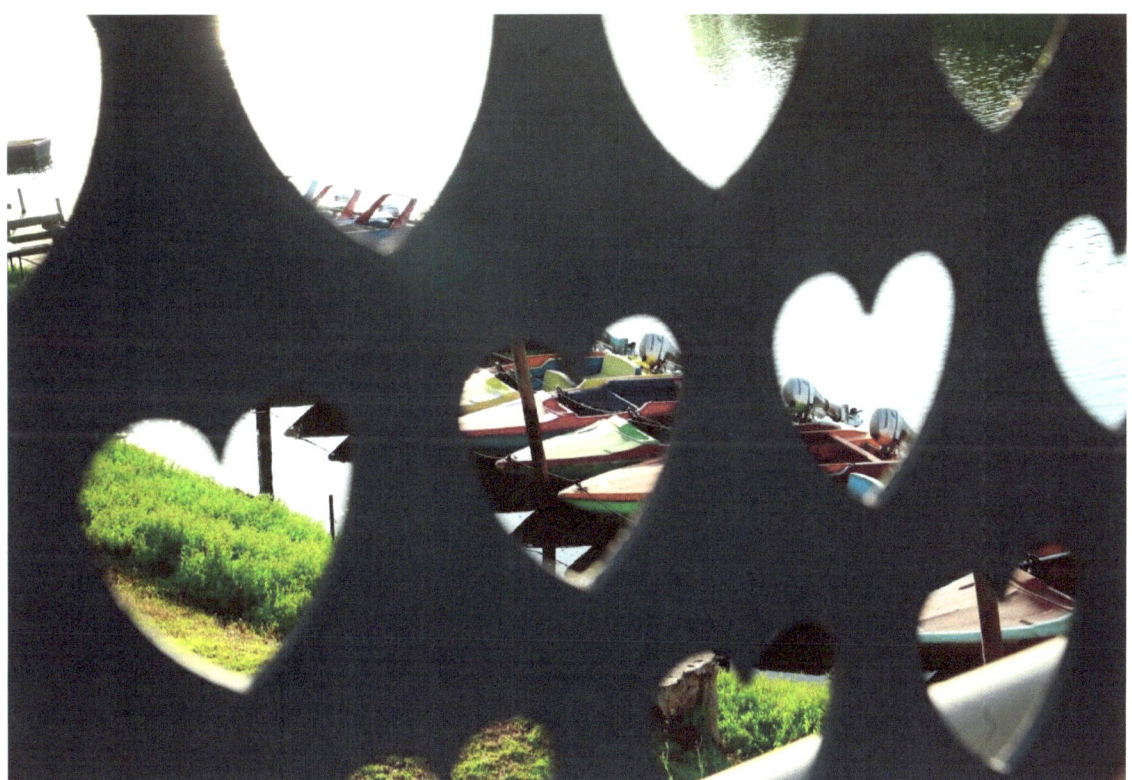

Exposure on the digital camera

While taking a photo the light sensors get exposed to light, this exposure is compiled by 2 parts: light brightness & duration of time it's on (light in picked up on sensors).

The brightness of light is controlled by the aperture (of lens), duration of light exposure is controlled by the shutter action. The size of the aperture opening related to the focal length of the lens (defined by 'F' & number);
Small aperture opening have large numbers: F-11, F-16
Large aperture opening have small numbers: F-4, F-5.6
The camera shutter opens & closes to expose the sensor to the light that crosses the aperture. Times of exposure are short term since the light sensors are sensitive to light (1/160 per second is a typical time frame).

*Note: Certain digital cameras offers vary shooting positions (shutter or aperture priority status), full manual option (all definitions are determined by the photographer & the camera performs without any auto-interference, correction etc.).

Exposure Compensation – Exposure Value (EV)

This function allows a fix to the amount of light auto determined by the camera during shooting (+/-). The exposure compensation is used to determine the camera's normal exposure level; you can brighten or darken the image.
In the case of major light contrasts such as light object on a dark backdrop, to get details of the light object you change the exposure (-2**..-1**..0..+1..+2) meaning less light during the shoot, as shown on function P (Under Exposure) Low Key.
In the case of a dark object on a lighter backdrop, to get details of the dark object you change the exposure level to 'more light' (-2..-1..0**..+1**..+2) in the photo than shown on function P (Over Exposure) High Key.

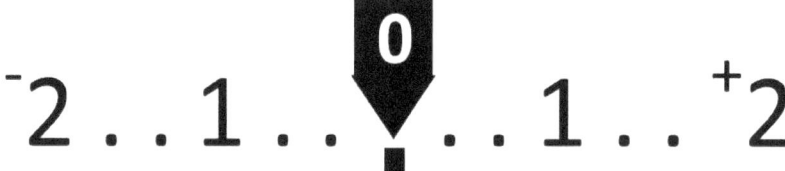

$^{-}2 .. 1 .. \blacktriangledown .. 1 .. ^{+}2$

Darker   **Lighter**

Graduated Auto-Exposure (Exposure Rate)

One click on the shoot button generates 3 photos shot at 3 different exposure states.

You can shoot one image of positive over exposure + negative over exposure + optimal state (0):

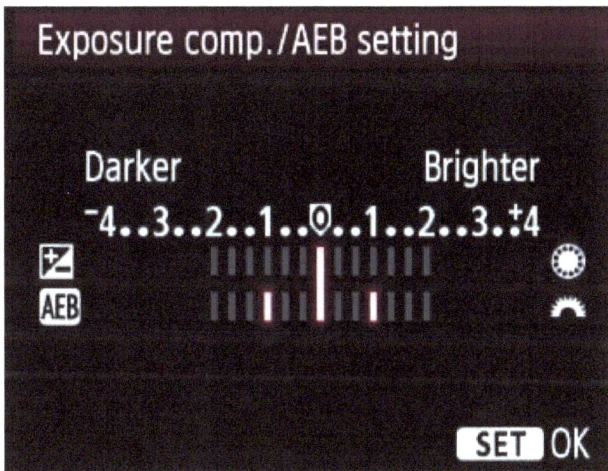

We will get 3 images:
1 brighter (+1)
1 darker (-1)
& 1 (0) much like function P standard exposure.

The series of images we will get: standard; exposure; decreased & increased.

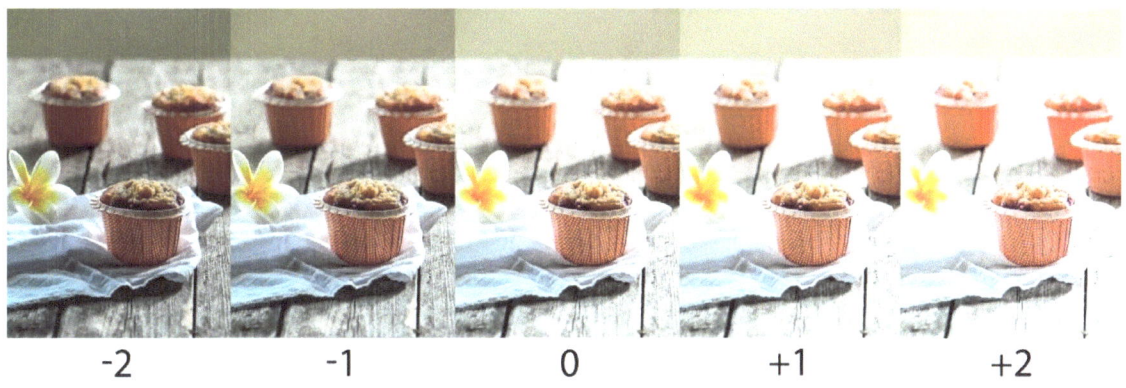

Photography Functions (BULB, Auto, M, TV, AV, P):

Auto – usually marked green, fully automated shooting.
Most functions (sequence speed, focus modes) are set automatically to prevent bad shooting, the photographer don't have any control over the different parameters of the camera, except for composition.

P Program – same as 'auto' state, but the photographer can change certain values: cancel the flash action, change ISO & close aperture. After the change the camera will configure the correct exposure for the shoot, a very convenient way to shoot fast & easy.

TV/S – Shutter Speed Priority
shutter speed priority happens when you turn the function selector button to TV/S state.
In this condition you can choose the shutter speed needed for the shoot. The speed is locked & the aperture adjusts itself to the chosen speed.

In some cameras the aperture number flickers (on the camera's control panel or on the bottom part of the screen) to indicate that the aperture speed is too low or too high. To reach the needed exposure you need to adjust the shutter speed until the aperture stops flashing.

Some cameras show the symbols 'LO' meaning shutter speed too high = under exposed, or 'HI' meaning shutter speed is too low = over exposure.

When you want to ensure prevention of blurring from the camera movements, you use speed of over 1/60 – 1/45 per second, below that speed its better if you use a tripod.

*Shutter speed 1/60, 1/120, 1/250, 1/500, 1/1000 etc.

AV/A – Aperture Priority:
Aperture priority happens when you turn the function selector button to A/AV, in this situation you can choose the needed aperture for the shoot. The aperture is locked & shutter speed adjusts itself to the chosen aperture.
In some cameras the number representing the shutter speed flashes to indicate that the shutter speed is too low or too high and you need to change the aperture opening until the shutter speed stops flashing.
To ensure sharpness of the objects in the photo its best to use high apertures F-11/F-16, and this way ensure that in any case the objects will be sharp enough.

*Aperture opening F-2.8, F-4, F-5.6, F-11, F-16

BULB – B – In markings B or T (M function on digital cameras), the shutter speed is very low, B or T function is to allow longer exposures than what the camera enables with the shutter speed. The use of function B is made by pressing the camera release.
The press will open the shutter which will remain open as long as you press the camera release, when you let go the shutter would close.

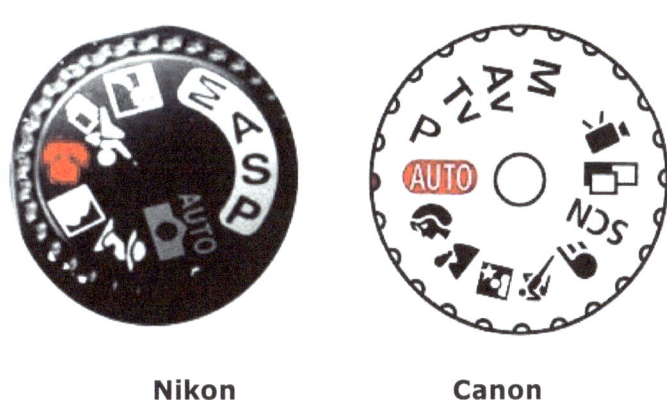

Nikon   **Canon**

INFLUENCIAL FACTORS OF DEPTH & SHARPNESS (Aperture opening changes):

When using a steady length focal point lens set to the same distance, you can see at the image below the sharpness depth changes with the changing aperture opening. The sharpness depth usually lasts about a third before the object & two thirds behind. The more the aperture opening is small the sharpness depth is large.

(F-2.8 aperture gives a shallow sharpness depth compared to F-22 aperture).

CAMERA DISTANCE:

The sharpness depth partially depends on the distance of the camera from the object of shooting. Even if all other lens directions are the same, as long as you go further away from the object of shooting (with the same exposure terms) the more the sharpness depth around the object grows.

Focusing on an object 5 meters away from the camera gives a larger sharpness depth than a 2 meters focus length.

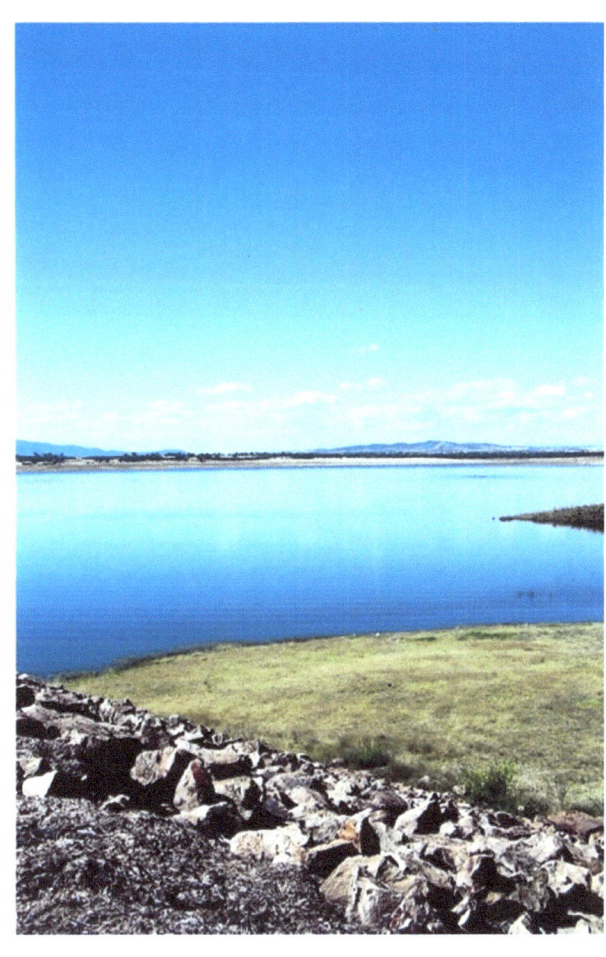
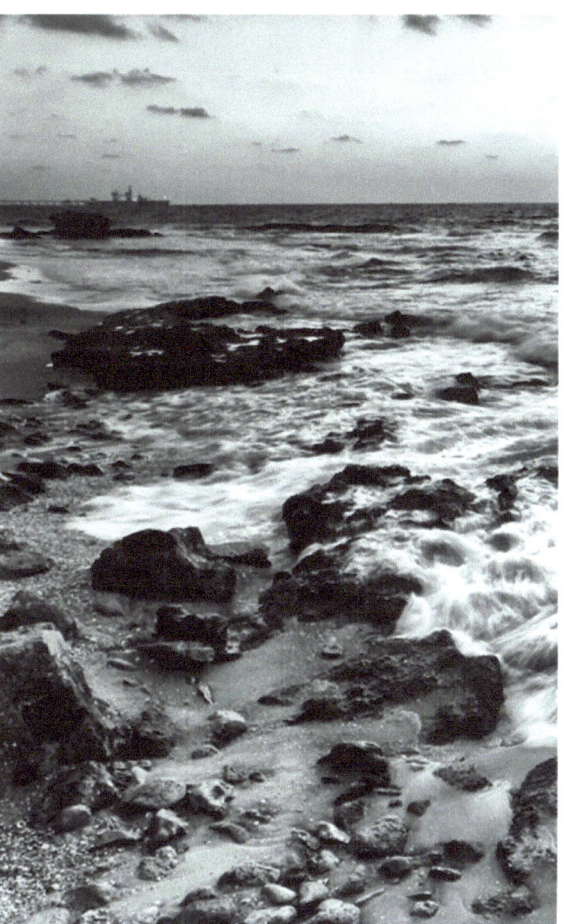
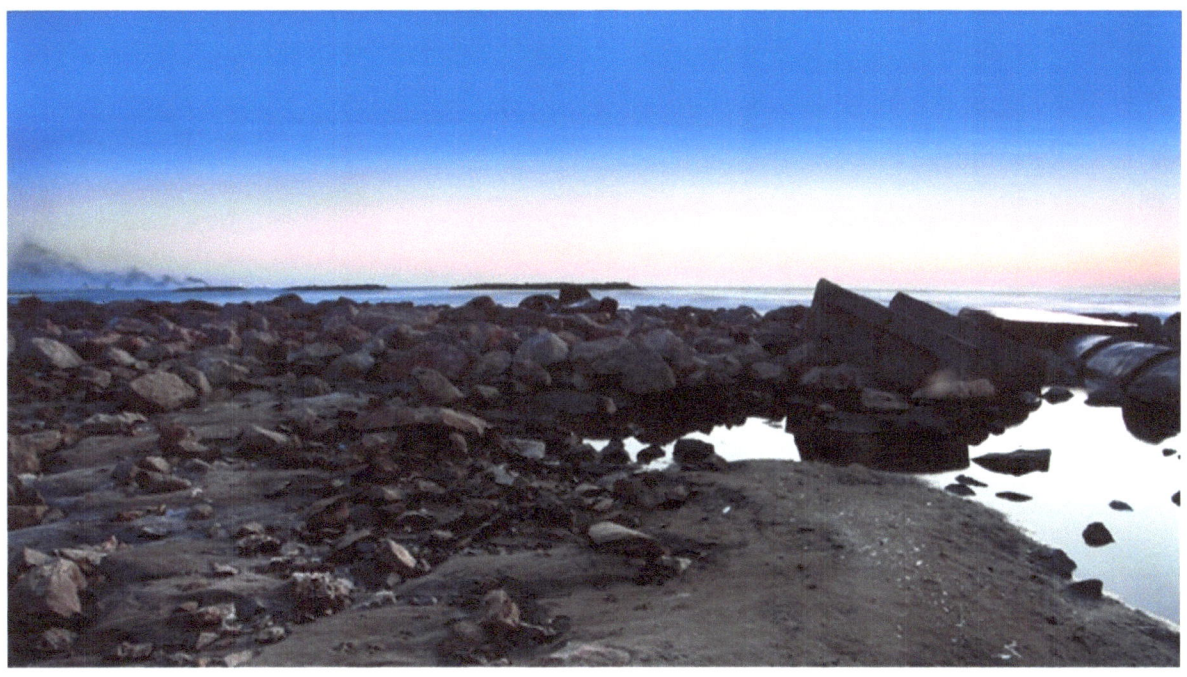

TYPES OF LENSES

ZOOM & STEADY FOCAL LENGTH LENSES   Zoom lens allows you to change the object size without moving the camera from its position, a trait that makes it very popular among photographers. Steady focal length lenses are of high quality & with a high depth of field.

When the object of shooting is at a set distance from the camera & you shoot with a similar aperture, you can change the sharpness depth (depth of field) by using a different focal point lengths lenses.
The more the focal length grows the smaller the sharpness depth we'll get. Focal length is a key factor with determining the sharpness depth (depth of field).
(*on a wide angle lens 8-15mm the depth of field is high on every aperture opening & there's hardly no need to focus it).

THE IMPORTANCE OF A LENS DIAMETER   One of the camera lens important trait is the diameter size of the lens, the amount & speed of light passing through it is affected by the diameter & this is a major factor in photography. The larger the lens diameter is, the amount of light passes through is larger. If we take 2 lenses with the same diameter but with a different focal length (50mm & 100mm), we will find that on the lens with a shorter focal length the amount of light passing through it will be larger. That's why this lens is defined faster (in addition you need to address the distance between the diameter & the sensor).

The calculation for finding the 'lens speed' is by dividing the lens focal length with the lens diameter size.

For example: a 50mm focal length with a lens diameter of 50mm, the lens speed will be:
1 – f = F/D = 50/50 or **Lens Speed = Length/Diameter**

F – focal length
D – lens diameter
f – lens speed

If the focal length is 50mm & the lens diameter is 25mm, the lens speed will be: **f = F/D 50/25 = 2** (the mark can appear as F=2 or 1:2).

WINDOW LIGHTING

Natural sun/daylight entering through the window (no direct sun), the light comes from one direction and since it's not a direct light it comes relatively scattered and with a certain direction (through window, balcony etc.). This kind of light Is very pleasant and easy to shoot portraits, food, products etc.

Diffused light (soft lighting) lights up the object usually in a unique manner which makes it easy to shoot. You can combine several exposure stages to receive a photo with ruling light/dark shades.

*By using flashes we can simulate the lighting nature.

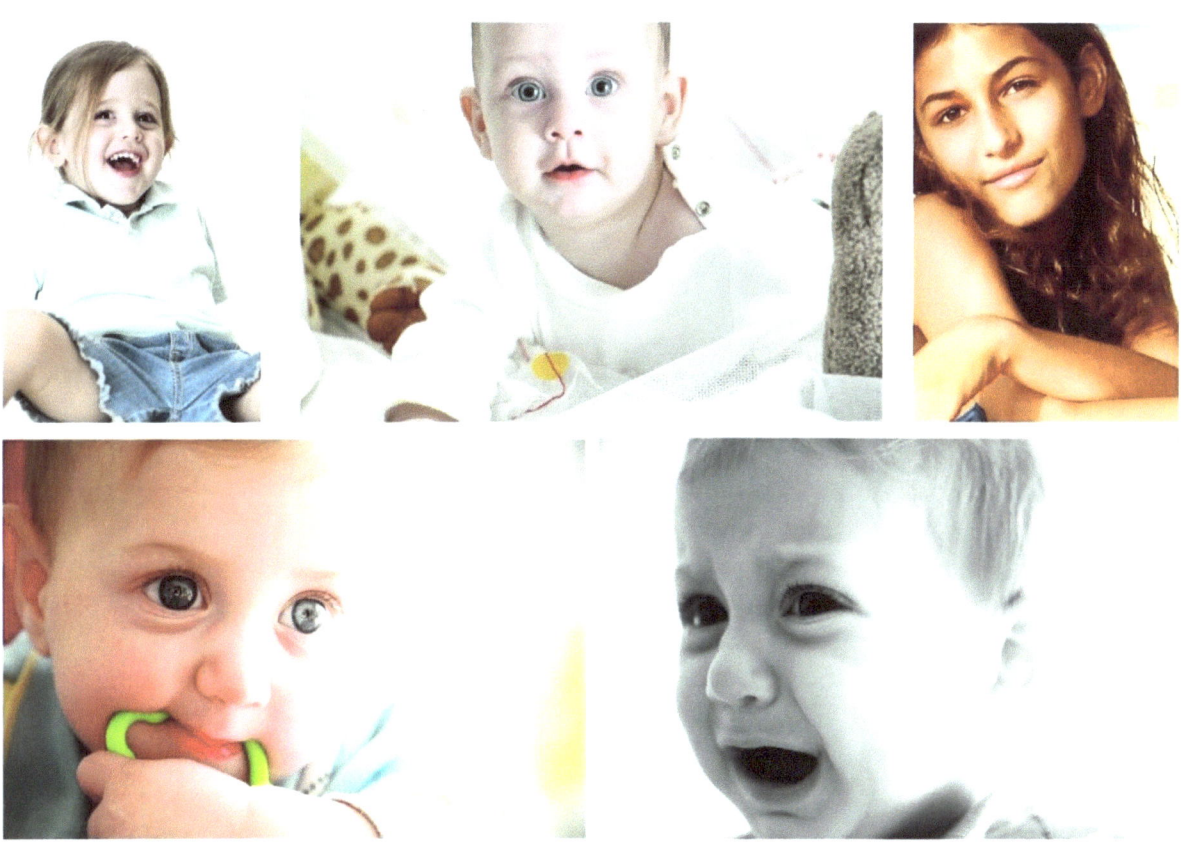

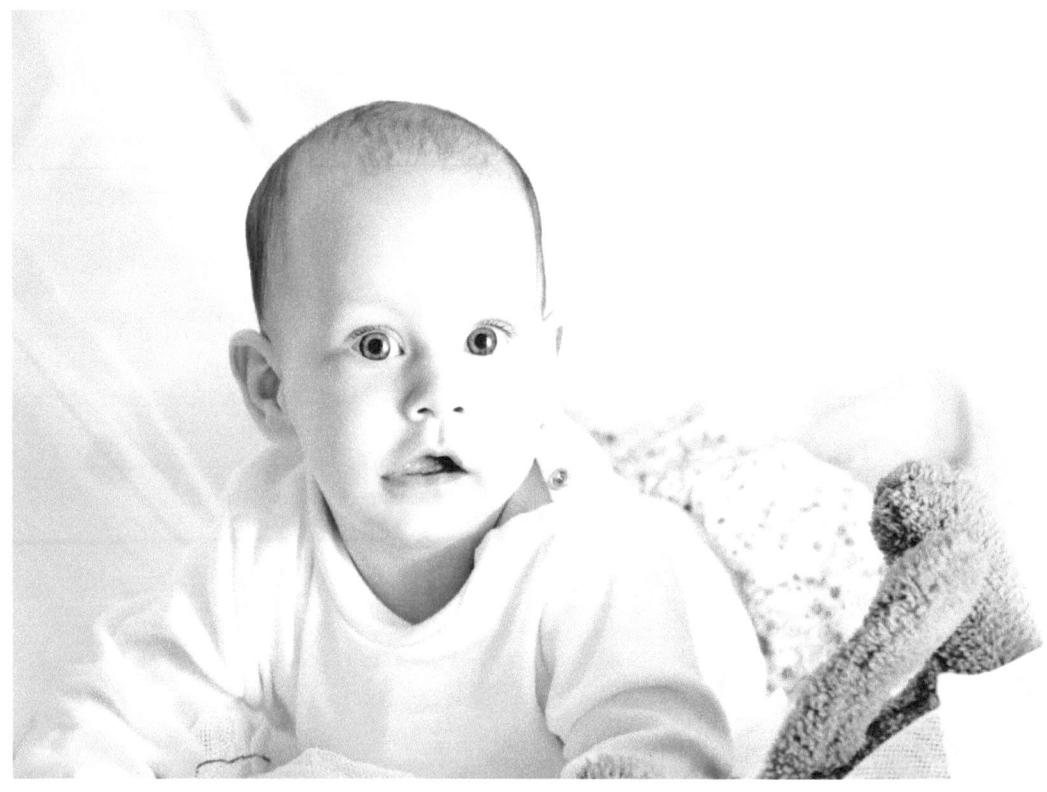

WINDOW LIGHT & PERFORMANCE OPTIONS

The object of shooting is located around 1-2 meters away from the light source (window, door, balcony etc.), according to the light intensity measure by P (Program) and adjusting the exposure accordingly.

When shooting portraits, you place the person at a 90/60/45 angles in order to get a high volume image with a sense of 3 dimension look.

When shooting a product (cup of coffee, flower vase etc.) or food, these can be placed across from the window. These shooting do not require flash use but do require a light reflector (a white surface backdrop/board, professional reflector) in order to shed light on the shaded areas that are opposite the light source.

LIGHT MEASURE

Light is the key factor influencing our photography, inside the camera there is a light meter return measuring the light reflected from the object of shooting.

The light meter is a sensor able to measure the amount of light entering through the lens & figuring the different indices needed for a correct exposure (shutter speed, aperture opening, ISO sensibility and use of flash). There are several ways to measure light – measuring the returning light & measuring the light fall:

Measuring the light fall:

Usually made by a light measure, used in professional photography, The light measure is by the object of shooting & during the shoot you can reach a precise accurate exposure (shutter speed & aperture opening), the light measure is a very easy accurate tool to achieve correct exposure in a photo.

Measuring returned light:

The measuring is made by the camera, there are several ways to measure light for example, when we half press the shoot button the light measure calculates how much light enters the lens & determine (in auto shooting) the right light exposure during the shoot.

LIGHT MEASURING OPTIONS

(Light measure with function P only)

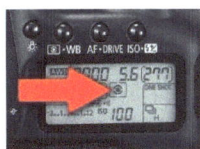

Specific Measuring: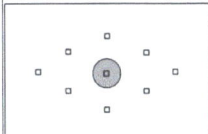

The light measure sizes up the light on the selected area only & recommends a correct suitable exposure.

Partial Measuring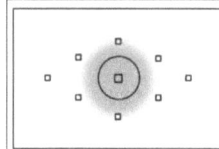

The light measure size up the selected area & adjust the exposure according the light in the area selected.

Weighted Measuring: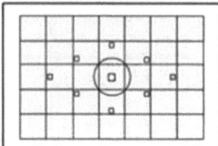

An average measuring referring to the general shooting area & adjusting the exposure according to the amount of light existing at the 75% of the frame (suitable for portrait photography).

Multipoint Measuring:

This measuring refers to a number of positions on the frame & calculates an average to the selected positions.

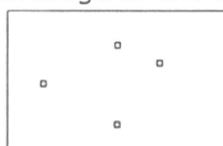

Formational Measure:

Formation light measuring is considered the best of all shooting situations; the camera divides the image to several areas & measures the light on each area, defining the correct exposure.

18% Grey Area Measuring:

This measure relates to the light bouncing back from the object of shooting, the assumption is that 18% of light is bouncing back from the object, by measuring a grey card placed by the object we will reach the correct exposure for the shoot.
Surfaces with different brightness levels will reflect different amounts of light therefor the measure will not be accurate enough; the grey card reflects an even amount of light which makes the measuring more accurate.

Blurring Measure:

To get an average exposure for our frame adjusting the camera to the object of shooting, move the lens to M position (manual focus) and blur the image until nothing is clear, half press the camera release button to run data (shutter speed & aperture opening) to M function, change back the lens, auto focus & shoot.

Measuring of a light/dark

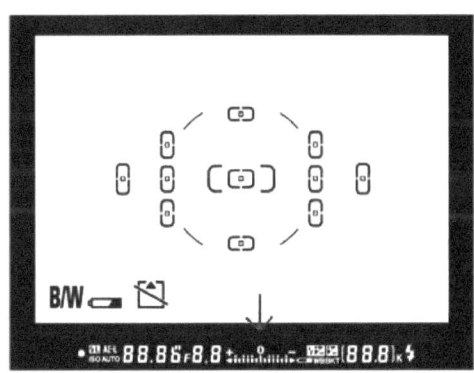

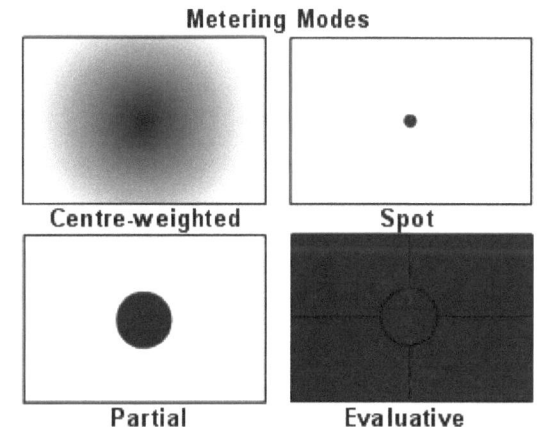

Surface:

In order to reach over-exposure (light shades rule) or under-exposure (dark shades rule) to measure of a white or black surface (on the shooting area), each touch will reach to an exposure with a light/dark shade rule.

CANON	NIKON
⊙ Evaluative metering	▦ Matrix
◎ Partial metering	
⊡ Spot metering	⊡ Spot
⊏⊐ Center-weighted average metering	▣ Center-weighted

CORRECT EXPOSURE

Correct exposure during shooting is the time of shoot needed (shutter speed) and the amount/intensity of light needed (aperture opening) to get the right exposure, a change in the closure or opening of the aperture changes the amount of light in the photo. The ratio between the light intensity to the shooting speed (exposure) is basically the ratio between the shutter to the aperture, a change in the opening of the aperture doubles the light amount F-4 F-5.6, a change in the shutter speed also doubles the light speed - 1/125 – 1/250, that is The reciprocal rule saying that the ratio between the shutter to the aperture is preserved even if we change (accordingly) the speed or aperture opening.

Correct exposure such as F-11 1/125 equals exposure F-8 1/250 We've opened one aperture (one stop) and closed (one stop) the shutter speed, therefor no change exposure wise. If we close another aperture and descend in shooting speed F-16 1/60 we will remain at the exact same exposure like F-11 1/125.

The interaction between shutter speed & aperture opening needs to remain according to this ratio.

Maintaining the interaction between shutter to aperture:

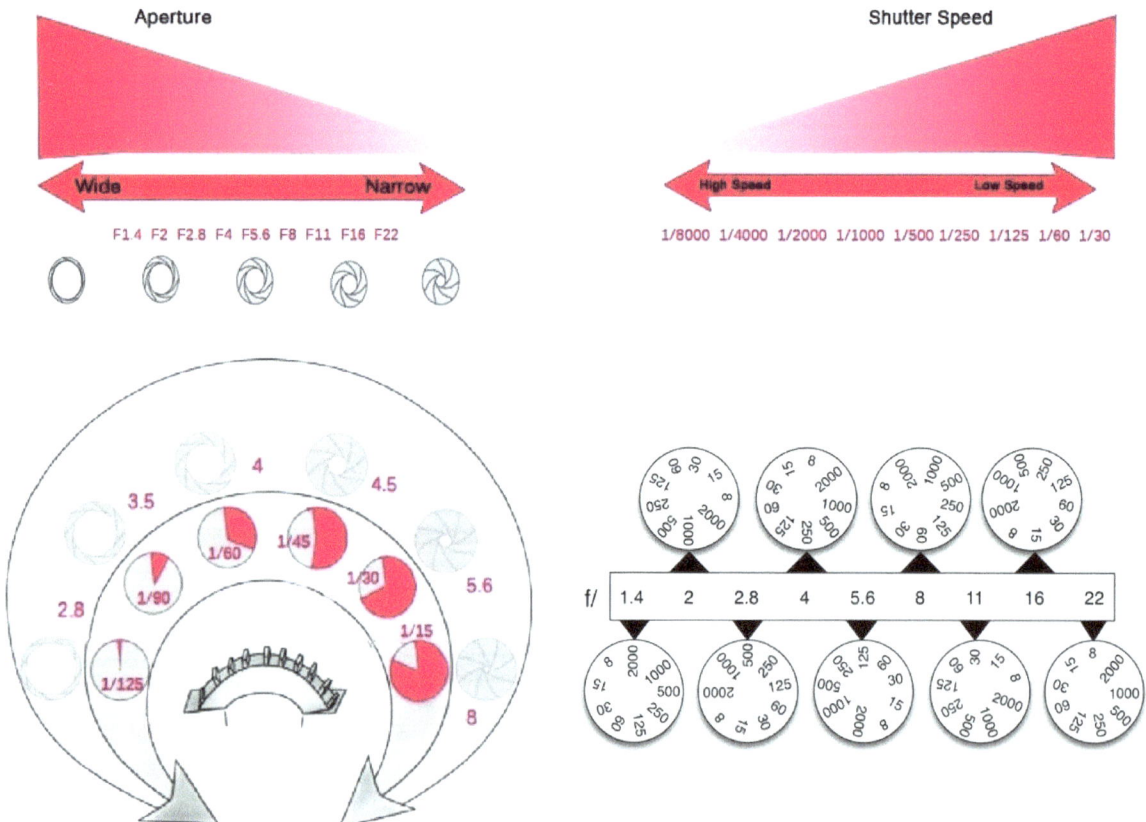

29

Aperture Openings:

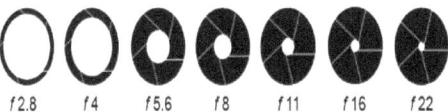

f 2.8   f 4   f 5.6   f 8   f 11   f 16   f 22

Shutter Speed (Closure):

1/8000 1/4000 1/2000 1/000 1/500 1/250
1/125 1/60 1/30 1/15 1/8 1/4 1/2 1 sec
2 sec 4 sec 8 sec 15 sec 30 sec 1 min
2 min 4 min 8 min 15 min 30 min 1 hour

DYNAMIC RANGE IMAGING (COLOR INTENSITY):

The human eye can detect dark details & light details even if the light intensity difference between them is high, a dynamic range is about the value (grey shades) between the lighter spot to the darker spot of the image.

In the sketch below you can spot the lighter parts (white color) and the darker area (black color), between these areas lies the brightness range of the camera sensor (remember it?), the larger the range is the more mid-tones/middle shades will appear, meaning more details in the lighter and the darker areas. To put it simply, the dynamic range for the sensor describes the difference between the minimal amount of light the sensor can detect to the most he can detect (with no opaque black areas to 'burnt' white areas).

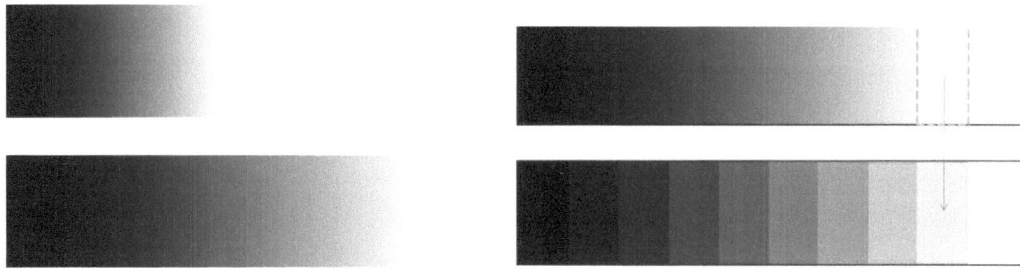

*A large dynamic range = many mid-tones, more details in both light & dark areas.

*A small dynamic range = smaller range of mid-tones, more 'burnt' light areas & opaque dark areas.

You can increase or decrease the dynamic range by exposure adjustment or by editing the image with graphic software ('LightRoom', 'Photoshop'). Another option is by changing the camera's contrast which increases or decreases the dynamic range of the image.

*For every photography problem there's a solution, you can change/adjust the focal method and reach better results, with Photoshop/LightRoom you can highlight the shadows or darken the lighter areas and by that reveal more details and get better exposure in most areas of the photo.

HDR – HIGH DYNAMIC RANGE PHOTOGRAPHY

Creating an image with a wide dynamic range is basically a technique that allows you to create an image containing details in both light & dark areas. Take for an example a photo of the beach – if we adjust the camera to over-exposure, certain areas will become burnt (the sun, the sky etc.), if we adjust for under-exposure, we will get over shaded dark areas (the sea, clouds), so you shoot the same photo (with a tripod or a steady surface) in different levels of exposure (remember? -2..-1..0..+1..+2) then join all different shoots into one photo through a photo processing software in option 'Merge to HDR'.

When using the HDR technique you can clearly see all the details in the photo, sometimes the use increases the dynamic range far from the dynamic range the human eye can see & gives you the sense as if the photo is unrealistic.

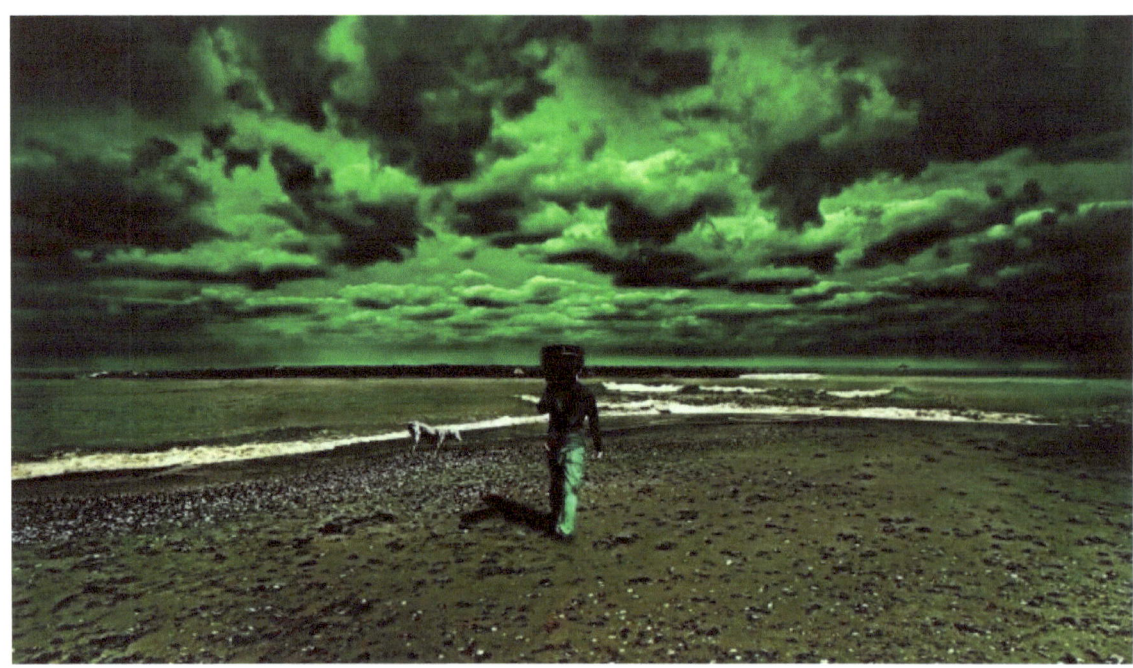

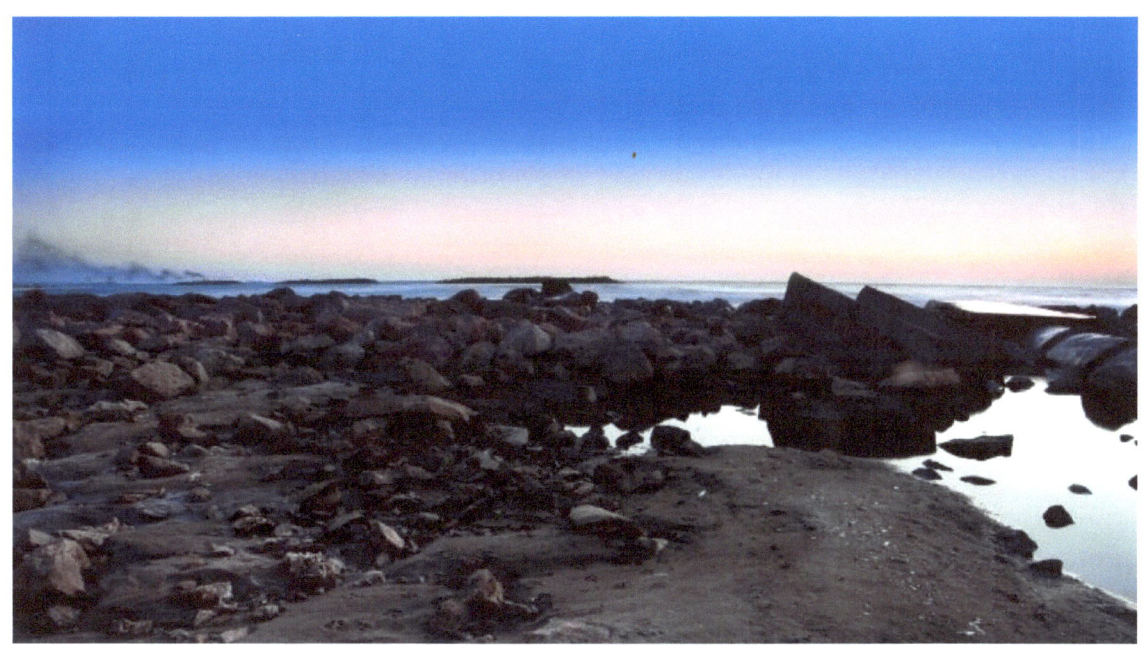

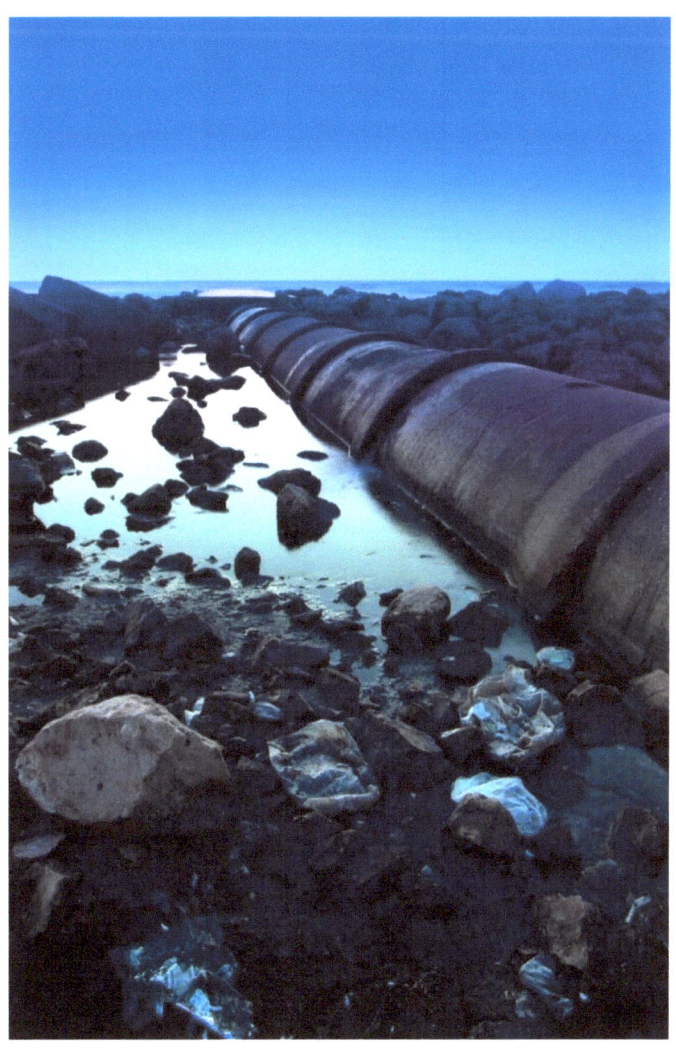

HDR Photography Rules:

Camera: The camera should allow automated graduate shooting, to adjust to (1+ 0 1-), you can shoot more than 3 images (2+ 1+ 0 1- 1-) try & see the difference.
It's best to shoot in RAW & not JPEG, the RAW files are flexible and the results are excellent.

Tripod: shooting with a tripod allow us to adjust composition & improve our shooting capabilities. There is a great importance to shooting with no change between images.

Lens: in this technique you usually shoot landscapes, sceneries & large areas so it's best to use a wide lens, plus a wide angle that gives a dramatic effect suitable to the nature of this technique.

Software: any graphic software that allow you to merge images (Photoshop is highly recommended), after the merge you can change certain parameters of the photo (color saturation, contrasts etc.) and achieve impressive results.

ISO: It's best to use low sensitivity (up to 200) to avoid noise & grain which harm the final photo.

Shoot the image at AV mode and choose aperture 8-11, it's important to shoot at this mode since the camera keeps an identical depth of field on all images.

Check that there aren't any moving objects on your frame, anything that moves will come up blurry on the photo. In case there a figure on the shoot make sure it won't move during the shooting (of all images), during the shoot make sure not to tilt or shake or move your tripod, in case there's a slight change it would be easier to fix later on Photoshop but it won't be easy to fix if your tripod is not steady, so shoot steady & quick.

An interesting angle creates an interesting image, take your time when setting compositions.

ASA – ISO

ASA is the American standard to measure sensitivity of the light sensor. The ASA is familiar to us since the age of film since American companies created photo films (Kodak). This regulation/standard is identical to the international standard – ISO, who took over the field since the majority of digital cameras is manufactured by Japanese companies (Sony, Olympus, Nikon, Canon etc.). The ISO standard is made to determine the sensitivity of the light sensor and what is the light amount necessary to achieve the right exposure.

Each sensor has its own sensitivity in which it performs best, the sensitivity is adjustable much like the aperture & shutter by jumping (stops) from low to high sensibility, each 'jump' doubles or reduces the sensitivity by half.

ISO sensibilities:

50, 100, 200, 400, 800, 1600, 3200, 6400, 12800, 25600 etc.

In general a large photo sensor allows higher amount of sensibility, size in this matter establish the amount of sensibility the camera can use and still maintain different components in the image and will not harm the quality. Know your camera & its limitations.

Usually ISO is measured in extreme light situations, the camera cannot produce great images when the lighting conditions are poor, here is when sensitivity and a good quality sensor comes in to play (usually on professional cameras) and produce better results than a small sensor that is usually installed on compact cameras and on some DSLR cameras. You don't have to run and purchase a professional camera, just be aware that in some situations the camera will not produce best results since it reached its limit.

Mostly this situation will occur during night shooting, where the lighting is not strong enough and a dark/shaded area on the image comes out 'noisy' and almost opaque which hurts the texture, the colors and in general hurting the final outcome. You can fix it a little with Photoshop and reach ok results.
The best way to know what are the limits of your camera's sensitivity is by shooting in low lighting conditions, shoot on several different sensitivity levels and view the results. The more the 'graininess' is gentle the sensitivity levels are lower, high sensitivity will hurt the textures of the details on the image.

The more the ISO is high the more sensitive the sensor will be and there will be 'noises' on the image (the pixels showing as grains on the photo).

In general its best to shoot with the lowest sensitivity possible that the shooting conditions allow, this will get us the best results and we will make the most out of our camera's quality. Another reason to raise the sensitivity is when a combination of the aperture and shutter that 'make' us hype up sensitivity.

End of Part 1 -
More Secrets, tips & ideas on Part 2

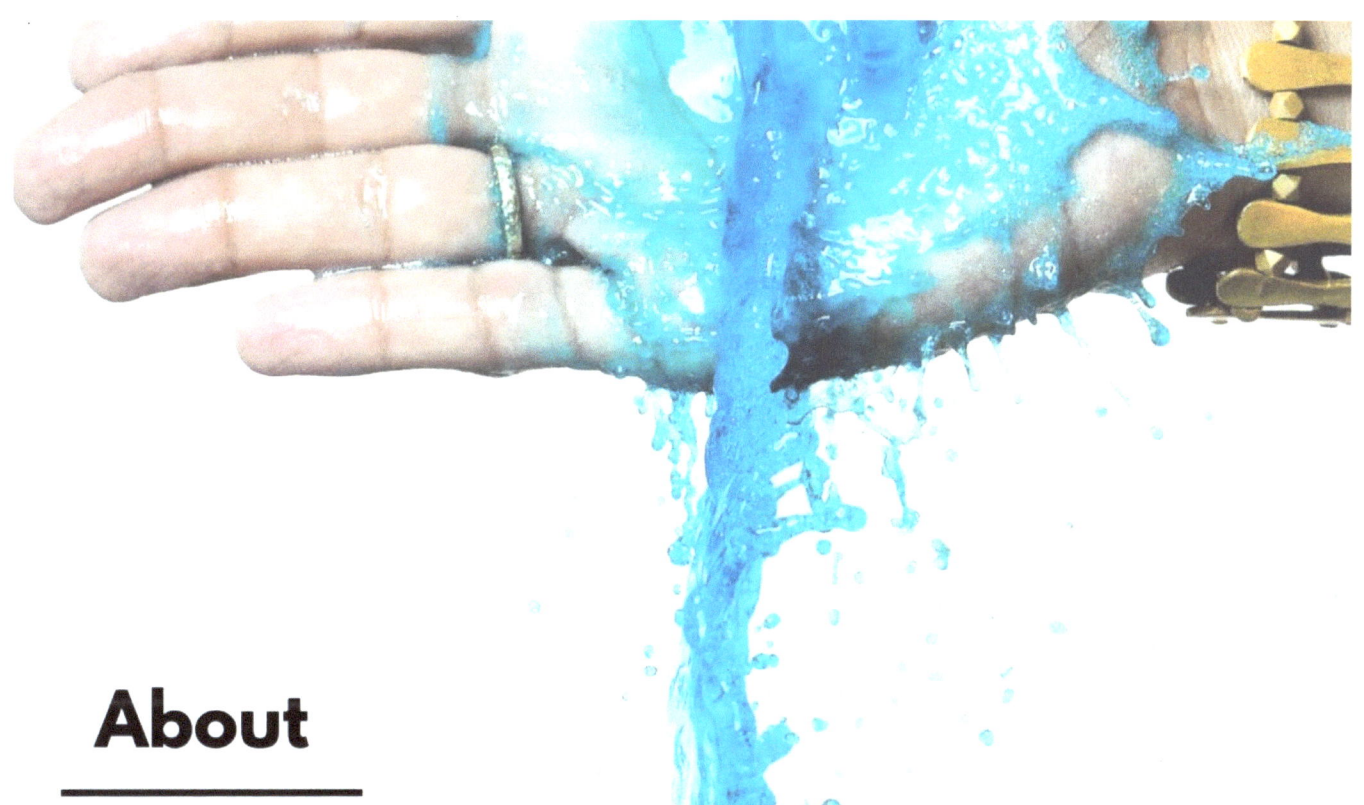

About

MY NAME IS TOMER & I'M LIVING THROUGH THE LENS FOR OVER A DECADE.

I SPECIALIZE IN GOURMET FOOD, PRODUCT & ARCHITECTURE PHOTOGRAPHY, I TOOK PART IN MANY SUCCESSFUL WORLDWIDE CAMPAIGNS & WORKED WITH SOME OF THE WORLD'S BIGGEST AGENCIES, MET SPECIAL CLIENTS, FASCINATING PEOPLE, BEEN TO MANY SPECTACULAR PLACES & MANY CREATIVE ADVENTURES THAT BECAME PART OF ME.

IN MY EBOOKS SERIES I'M SHARING WITH YOU SOME OF THE SECRETS, TIPS & TECHNIQUES I'VE PRACTICED & USED TO BECOME WHAT I AM, AND I HOPE IT WILL HELP YOU TOO.

www.ingramcontent.com/pod-product-compliance
Lightning Source LLC
Chambersburg PA
CBHW041318180526
45172CB00004B/1147